ISBN 978-0-331-88146-2
PIBN 11040034

PREFACE.

collection of·Old English Country Dances is a modest attempt to bring before the public to-day some few simple dance tunes which amused former generations. The musician judge the tunes from a modern standpoint, but probably he will find amongst them many l repay his attention. To a musical antiquary little need be said, for he will know that lish dance music is especially interesting in many ways, one of which is the light it throws evolution of numbers of our popular airs; and in this volume the editor has attempted to e growth of the tune, "The Keel Row," from an earlier source than has been before set The dances having Yorkshire titles will, perhaps, interest antiquaries of that county. The n consists not of the most popular, but of the least known, country dances having merit, selected to show the variety of styles in vogue from the middle of the 17th to the beginning 19th century. Many of the dances are from MSS. in the editor's possession, and in some ces have never before been printed, but may have been noted down in MS. from some

itinerant performer. The small oblong shape has been used for the work as the traditiona
country dance books. The notes at the end are original matter, and it is hoped may
interesting. It is trusted, too, that the bibliography of country dance music will be u
collectors. The list is, of course, necessarily very imperfect, and can only be rendere
complete by outside help. The editor hopes that this will be forthcoming, and will gladly w
additions.

Many beautiful Irish and Scottish airs of a similar class to those given here, remain bu
old printed collections, inaccessible to the general public, and a selection from these is intend
put forth at a later period. The editor also purposes to issue a collection of Traditional
Tunes hitherto unpublished, and he will be glad to hear from persons living in remote di
where such relics still linger, and who could contribute to such a gathering.

128, BURLEY ROAD, LEEDS.

CONTENTS.

CONTENTS.

THE KING'S DELIGHT.

THE 29TH OF MAY.

LORD FROG AND LADY MOUSE.

THE FROG AND THE MOUSE.

THE LUCKY HIT.

RED HOUSE.

PUNCH ALIVE.

THE BASHFUL SWAIN.   WINDSOR TERRACE.

THE DAME OF HONOUR.   FROM THEE TO ME SHE TURNS HER EYES.

CULLODEN FIGHT.   CURE OF ALL GRIEF.

GE HO, DOBBIN.

TWO AND TWO.

THE HEREFORDSHIRE LASSES.

POT STICK.

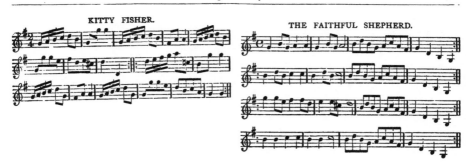

KITTY FISHER.

THE FAITHFUL SHEPHERD.

SPITHEAD FLEET.

WELCOME TO ALL STRANGERS.

CAPTAIN DRIVER'S DELIGHT.

THE WEDDING RING.

THE GROVE.

THE BALL. YANKY DOODLE.

VAN ROTTERDAM OP DORT.   THE RUNAWAY.

COME ASHORE, JOLLY TAR, YOUR TROUSERS ON.

YORKSHIRE GREY.

MERRY WAKEFIELD.   SCARBOROUGH WHIM.

YORKSHIRE LAD.

SMILING POLLY.

THE DUMB GLUTTON.   ### WELL MAY THE KEEL ROW.

HUMP MY LADY.   THE TIDE COME IN.

DOWN THE WAGGON WAY.

WE MUST ALL WAIT TILL MY LADY COMES HOME.

O! THE WEARY WATERS OF TYNE.

NEW ROAD TO ALSTON.

THE PLAINS OF WATERLOO.

NUMBER ONE.

THE FOGGY DEW.

MISS BAKER'S HORNPIPE.

THE KIRKGATE HORNPIPE.—*First Version.*

THE KIRKGATE HORNPIPE.—*Second Version.*

A Y ME, OR THE SYMPHONY, Page 1.—This very beautiful air deserves to be better known ; Chappell is silent about it. It is evidently the tune to some plaintive ditty of the 17th century, which I have not been able to meet with. It appears in many editions of the *Dancing Master ;* in the first, 1651 ; in the second, 1652 ; and the third to the eighth, 1690.

IF ALL THE WORLD WERE PAPER, Page 1.—Many Nursery Rhymes are, as most people are aware, extremely old, both in respect to the words and to the air, and though fragments of the rhymes occur frequently in early MSS., and in old printed books, yet it is seldom the tunes ever got into print. There are, however, several such airs in Playford's *Dancing Master,* and this is one of them. It appears in the first edition, 1651, and in other editions, including the eighth, 1690. It is arranged as a round dance for eight persons. The words of the rhyme are well known, and run thus—

> " If all the world were paper,
> And all the sea were ink?
> And all the trees were bread and cheese,
> What should we do for drink?

There is an Irish tune in Crosby's *Irish Musical Repository,* and in Smith's *Irish Minstrel,* named "If the sea were ink," but it is quite different to the one here printed.

ONCE I LOVED A MAIDEN FAIR, Page 1.—I give this air chiefly to show the difference which exists between it in the original form, and the air which Chappell has made so very popular. I do not claim for it that it is any better, nor even so good, but a copy direct from the earliest book, in which it was printed, may be interesting. It is taken from the *Dancing Master*, first edition, 1651, and it occurs in exactly the same notation in Playford's *Introduction in the Skill of Musick.* and in other of Playford's publications. Chappell mentions that it also occurs in the *Pleasant Companion for the Flageolet*, 1680. This latter work I have not seen. Chappell's version has a great resemblance to "Here's a Health unto his Majesty," by Saville. The original ballad sung to "Once I loved a maiden fair" is in the Roxburghe collection.

THE 29TH OF MAY, Page 2.—An exceedingly fine and marked air of Charles the Second's time. It first appears in the *Dancing Master*, in 1686, and is continued through the later editions. In the additional sheet, printed in 1698, the air is given and named "The Jovial Beggars."

THE KING'S DELIGHT, Page 2.—From Playford's *Introduction to the Skill of Musick*, 14th edition, 1700, and possibly in earlier editions of the same work. It is in "*Musick's Handmaid*," 1678, and is also noted down in a manuscript volume of airs, known as "Agnes Humes' MS, in the Advocate's Library, Edinburgh;" this MS. bears the date 1704. It is a good and lively tune, and was adopted by John Gay, for a song, in the *Beggar's Opera*, 1728. "The Gamesters and Lawyers are Jugglers alike." Previous to Gay's song it had been used as the air for a not over refined song. The first line of this is given in the early editions of the opera, as the original name of the air, but it will not bear repetition. It is also used in Arnold's opera, "Two to One," 1784.

LORD FROG AND LADY MOUSE, Page 3.—This is sometimes called "Cocky mi Chari, She," from the chorus of a song, in D'Urfey's *Fills*, vol. 1. It is said to be the original of "Muirland Willie." As "Lord Frog," it is in

Walsh's Dances for 1713, and either under the first or second title in several ballad operas. The present set is from Gay's opera "*Achilles*," 1733.

THE FROG AND MOUSE, Page 4.—This air is one of the many adapted to the Nursery Song, "A frog he would a wooing go." The original ballad boasts a somewhat high antiquity. In 1549, it is mentioned in the "*Complaint of Scotland*," as "The frog cam to the myl dur" [mill-door], and, according to Chappell, a ballad "Of a most strange wedding of a frog and mouse," was entered at Stationer's Hall, in 1584. In 1611, the song with music is inserted in "*Melismata*,' and in 1719, in "*Pills to Purge Melancholy*," a political song, founded upon it, was written by Tom D'Urfey. The air here printed is from "*Thompson's Pocket Companion for the German Flute*," 1797. It is the same air as that used for the song "Amo Amas, I love a lass," in the *Agreeable Surprise*, 1781. The air now generally sung to "A frog he would a wooing go," was by C. E. Horn.

THE LUCKY HIT, P. 4 —This quaint little tune is undoubtedly old. It appears in Watt's edition of "The Fashionable Lady, or Harlequin Opera," acted and printed 1730. The title, "The Lucky Hit" is the old name of the tune, a song being adapted to it in the opera. John Watt's editions of the old ballad operas are of great use to the musical antiquary, as the airs for the song are not only given, but the old names of the ballads and songs which were sung to them before being used for the opera. These are of value in tracing the airs through their many changes.

RED HOUSE, Page 4.—This tune is worthy of notice as the original germ from whence the song—"D'ye ken John Peel" sprung. The story is to the effect that the writer of the song, "John Peel," adapted his words to an air, which was sung to send his child to sleep by its granny. This was "Whar wad bonny Anne lie," or "Whar wad our guidman lie." This Scotch air is almost identical with Red House. Red House was in favour in the early part of the 18th century, and was greatly used in the ballad operas of the day, and as a country dance. It is found in the *Dancing Master*, 12th edition, 1703 and 1716 ; in Walsh's *Dancing Master*, 1719, &c. ; in *Polly*, 1729 ; *Lover's Opera*, 1730 ; *Fashionable Lady*, 1720, &c.

PUNCH ALIVE, Page 4. – From the third volume of Playford's *Dancing Master*, 1728.

BASHFUL SWAIN, Page 5.—From the same.

WINDSOR TERRACE, Page 5.—Or as it is more frequently spelt Windsor Tarass, is the air to a song by D'Urfey, in vol. 1. of "*Pills*."

> "Musing, I late, on Windsor Tarass sate,
> And hot and weary, heard a merry
> Amorous couple chat.
> *   *   *   *
> He had shown her all the lodgings great and small,
> The Tower, the Bower, the Green, the Queen,
> And famed St. George's Hall," &c.

It is printed in 16th edition of Playford's "*Dancing Master*," 1716, and in the "*Fashionable Lady*," 1730, also in vol. III. of *Thompson's Country Dances*. There in an air called "Windsor Tarris," in Walsh's "*Compleat Country Dancing Master*," 1714, but it by no means resembles the foregoing. The air here printed is good and peculiar, and persons conversant with Welsh music will readily recognise in it the original of the "*Dawning of the Day*."

FROM THEE TO ME SHE TURNS HER EYES, Page 6.—A good melody, used for a song in the ballad opera, the '*Fashionable Lady, or Harlequin Opera*," 1730. "From thee to me," &c., is the first line of an early song which I have not found, nor have I seen another copy of the air. The first part of the tune appears to have suggested the opening strain of "The Dusky Night rides down the Sky."

THE DAME OF HONOUR, Page 6.—Is frequently called "Queen Bess' Dame of Honour." It is the air for a capital song by, I believe, Thomas D'Urfey, and was sung by Mrs. Willis, in the opera, "The Kingdom of the Birds." It is to be seen in "*Pills to Purge Melancholy*," 1719, vol. I., and commences :—

> "Since now the world's turned upside down,
> And all things changed in Nature ;
> As if a doubt were newly grown,
> We had the same Creator
> Of ancient modes and former ways,
> I'll teach you, sirs, the manner
> In good Queen Bess' golden days,
> When I was dame of honour."

The air soon became a great favourite, and was used in many ballad operas as "*Polly*," 1729 ; *Fashionable Lady*, 1730 ; The *Lottery*, 1731 ; The *Devil to Pay*, 1731 ; *Jovial Crew*, 1732 ; and in the *Dancing Master*, vol. II., 1728.

CULLODEN FIGHT, Page 7.—From Johnson's "200 favourite Country Dances, vol. 4th, 1748 ;" also in Longman,

Lukey, & Co.'s Dances for 1772. Soon after the 1745 rebellion, some military officers having called upon the musicians at the Canongate Theatre, Edinburgh, for this air, and the rest of the audience having demanded "You're Welcome, Charlie Stuart," a serious riot ensued.

CURE OF ALL GRIEF, Page 7.—From Johnson's Country Dances, vol. IV., 1748.

GE HO, DOBBIN! Page 8 —This has ever been a most popular air, and a countless number of humorous songs have been set to it. It being a good and catching melody, with a refrain which every body knew, caused it so largely to be employed. The original song is called—"The Waggoner, or Ge ho, Dobbin!" and is in *Apollo's Cabinet*, or the *Muses Delight*, 1757.—

> "As I was a driving my waggon one day,
> I met a young damsel tight—buxom and gay;
> I kindly accosted her with a low bow,
> And I felt my whole body I cannot tell how;
> Ge ho, Dobbin! Hi ho Dobbin!
> Ge ho, ge Dobbin! Ge ho, ge ho!" &c.

There are eight verses. The present copy (with the terminal strain added from *Apollo's Cabinet*), is from *Thompson's Country Dances*, vol. I., *circa* 1759. A song in "*Love in a Village*," 1762, is set to this air. The modern tune has considerable difference from this original one, and is frequently published.

TWO AND TWO, Page 8.—A somewhat singular air, taken from *Thompson's Collection of Country Dances for* 1763.

HEREFORDSHIRE LASSES, Page 9.—A very pretty air, found in Longman, Lukey, & Co.'s Country Dances, for 1772.

· POT STICK, Page 9.—This is the earliest copy of the air, "Over the Water to Charlie," I have seen. It is taken from Johnson's 200 *Country Dances*, vol. IV., 1748. After this date, the air appears under the Irish title—"Shambuie," or "Shamboy," in "*Thompson's Country Dances*," vol. I., circa 1759; in Oswald's "*Caledonian Pocket Companion*," vol. II., and in other collections. In Aird's *Selection of English and Foreign Airs*, vol. I., circa 1775-6, it is named "The Marquis of Granby," from a song by G. A. Stevens. The tune also has another name in Irish Collections, "Ligrum Cush," or "Lacrum Cosh," in *Hime's Dances*, and in *Holden's Irish Airs*. Robt. Burns, in a letter to Geo. Thomson, mentions this name as a title given to the old Scotch melody, "The Quaker's Wife." Whether the tune be English, Scotch, or Irish, would be a difficult matter to settle, but, certainly, at an early period the song, "Over the water to Charlie," was set to it, and under this title it is inserted in vol. I. of the *Caledonian Pocket Companion*, Book 4, circa 1755, and in Bremner's Reels, circa 1759. In Gow's 3rd Collection of Strathspeys it has yet another name given it—"Wishaw's Delight."

KITTY FISHER. Page 10.—An air named in honour of this notorious lady. From "*Thompson & Son's Twenty-four Country Dances, for* 1760."

FAITHFUL SHEPHERD, Page 10.—A quaint air, in "*Thompson's Complete Collection of Country Dances . . . for the Harpsichord, circa* 1775." It is also in Aird's Selection, vol. I., and here the last bar of each strain is G, B, D, G ascending.

SPITHEAD FLEET, Page 11.—An air of considerable merit, greatly reminding one of certain Scottish tunes, with a termination more Irish in character. From Peter Thompson's "200 *Country Dances*," circa 1759.

WELCOME TO ALL STRANGERS, Page 11.—From McGlashan's "*Scots' Measures*," circa 1780.

CAPTAIN DRIVER'S DELIGHT, Page 12.—In Johnson's "200 *Country Dances*," vol. IV., 1748.

THE GROVE, Page 12.—From McGlashan's "*Scots' Measures.*"

THE WEDDING RING, Page 12.—From No. 8 of "*Dale's Collection of Reels and Dances,*" folio, *circa* 1806.

THE BALL, Page 13.—A good and sprightly air, which seems to have first seen the light in "*Fourteen favourite Cotillion and Country Dances. . . . The Fifteenth Book, for the year* 1786. . . Thomas Budd." Oblong 16mo.

YANKY DOODLE, Page 13.—The history of the National Air of America is involved in much obscurity, and many absurd statements have been made regarding it, but for a very able article dealing with the subject, by Mr. Barclay Squire, I must refer the reader to Grove's *Dictionary of Music.* Dr. Rimbault's states that the air is printed in Walsh's Dances, for 1750, as "Fisher's Jig." Though I have seen earlier years of Walsh's yearly collections, I have not seen the one in question and am unable to verify the matter. In 1784, in George Colman's Opera—"Two to One," (the music selected and arranged by Dr. Arnold, the title says "composed," but as the airs include "Peg of Derby," "King's Delight," "Duncan Gray," and other Scotch airs, this is absurd) there is a song "Adzooks Old Crusty, why so rusty?" and the music for this is "Yankee Doodle." Mr. Squire thinks this is probably the earliest appearance of the air in print, but, I believe the set I now give is, at least, eight or nine years previous. It is from "*A Selection of Scotch, English, Irish, and Foreign Airs. . . . Glasgow,* James Aird, vol. I." Oblong 16mo. It is unfortunately not dated, but I cannot find any air in it which gives a later date than 1775 or 1776, and I fix its publication at about that period. It ultimately extended to six volumes, and there are, at least, three different editions, one a late one, published by G. Goulding, London, *circa* 1785. The later volumes were published long after the first. In the first there is a Negro Jig, and several "Virginian Airs." The tune "Yanky Doodle" has here several variations which I have not reprinted.

VAN ROTTERDAM OP DORT, Page 14.—This, perhaps, should not have a place in the collection, for it is evidently as its name implies a Dutch air. But, as it is found in an English dance book, and is pleasing, it is reproduced from Straight and Skillern's Dances for 1774.

THE RUNAWAY, Page 14.—From a manuscript, written about 1825. It is different to a dance with this title which appears in dance books at the commencement of the century.

COME ASHORE, JOLLY TAR, Page 15.—This lively air is in "*A Selection of English, Irish, and Foreign Airs, adapted for the Fife, Violin, and German Flute.* Glasgow, James Aird, vol. I." Aird's selection, which extended to six volumes, and of which, at least, three different editions are known, is an exceedingly good and curious work. It was published at the end of the last century, the first being printed some time about 1775 or 1776. In the "*Jacobite Relics,*" first series, 1819, James Hogg gives a song to this air, commencing :—

> "The cuckoo's a bonny bird when he comes home,
> The cuckoo's a bonny bird when he comes home ;
> He'll fley away the wild birds that hank about the throne,
> My bonny cuckoo when he comes home."

Regarding this air, he says:—"It must have been a great favourite in the last age, for about the time when I first began to know one tune from another, all the old people that could sing at all, could sing, 'The cuckoo is a bonny bird.'" The present copy of the air is taken from a manuscript, dated "Falkirk, 1824." It is a slightly better set than either Aird's or Hogg's.

YORKSHIRE GREY, Page 15.—In "*Thompson's Complete Collection of Country Dances and Cotillions for the Harpsichord*," C. and S. Thompson, oblong 8vo., *circa* 1775. The first part appears to have been suggested by "Hunting the Hare," or the "Green Gown."

MERRY WAKEFIELD, Page 16.—From "*Rutherford's Complete Collection of the Most Celebrated Country Dances, both old and new. . . . printed by David Rutherford*," no date, *circa* 1775. The epithet "Merry" has been applied to Wakefield from time immemorial, and there are many very old songs in which this term is used.

THE SCARBOROUGH WHIM, Page 16.—Another dance named in honour of a Yorkshire town, it is like the above in *Rutherford's* Collection, and I have not seen it reprinted.

THE MERRY GIRLS OF YORK, Page 17.—From "*A Collection of Scots' Measures, Hornpipes*," &c. Alex. Mc. Glashan, Edinburgh; oblong folio, *circa* 1780. The same dance is inserted in Hodsall's Country Dances for 1810. It is there called "Harrogate Lodge."

THE YORKSHIRE BITE, Page 17.—This tune is from Twenty-four Dances for 1788, published by T. Skillern.

THE YORKSHIRE LAD, Page 18.—From Johnson's Country Dances, 1748. See "Well may the Keel Row," below.

SMILING POLLY, Page 18.—From Thompson's Dances for 1763. See "The Keel Row."

DUMB GLUTTON, Page 19.—From Aird's Selection, vol. I., *circa* 1775.

WELL MAY THE KEEL ROW, Page 19.—There has lately been much controversy as to whether this be a Scotch or a Northumbrian Air, and the dispute puts one in mind of the old fable of the parti-colored shield, as each set of disputants has some right on its side. It is, in my opinion, a futile task to attempt to definitely settle the birth-place of a particular air, for a good melody soon travels even a longer way than from Scotland to Northumberland, or *vice versa*, and as it was the case in old times, that the air was carried by fiddlers and persons totally unacquainted with notation, or the "pricking" down of melodies, the characteristic of each country was implanted on it, carried as it was only by ear. In the "Yorkshire Lad" we have, as far as I have been able to find, the earliest germ of the melody the "Keel Row." The first named is in a London dance book (Johnson's Collection) in 1748, and as this was a gathering together of a series of dances which had been published annually, I have no doubt it could be found in print even earlier than 1748. Following this, we find in Thompson's yearly dances for 1763, "Smiling Polly," which is virtually the same as the "Yorkshire Lad," and to show that this first strain of the "Keel Row" is common to many early country dances, I print the "Dumb Glutton" from Aird's "Selection," *circa* 1775; and others might also have been given which are distinctly like the air, viz., "Shamboy Breeches," in Stewart's

Reels, *circa* 1770. "Charlie is at Edinburgh," in a MS., &c. The earliest appearance in print of the tune named as the "Keel Row," is in "*A Collection of favourite Scots' Tunes, with Variations for the Violoncello or Harpsichord, by the late Charles McLean, and other eminent masters,*" printed at Edinburgh, by N. Stewart, oblong 4to, pp. 37. not dated, but assigned in the British Museum Library to the date 1770, and in Dr. Laing's Bibliography of Scottish Collections to 1776. I have seen the work advertised on a book bearing the engraved date 1780. In Mc. Lean's collection the tune is named "Well may the Keel Row," and is now reproduced in this present volume. I am not inclined to lay much stress on the fact that, because it appears in a Scotch collection, it is necessarily Scottish, for although of the twenty-six airs in Mc. Lean's collection, there are twenty-one which certainly few would dispute (the rest being Irish, except the Keel Row), yet it was the practice to include in such like collections any tune good and popular. In Cromek's *Remains of Nithsdale and Galloway Song*, 1810, which was certainly *not all* Allan Cunningham's fabrications, it is called a "popular bridal tune in Scotland," and has the Jacobite Song, "As I came down the Cannogate," set to it. If this be a genuine Jacobite effusion, and I certainly see no reason to doubt it, Cunningham's Song, "Merry may the Keel Rowe," in vol. III. of his "*Songs of Scotland,*" 1825, is evident as a copy of the old song: it is thus :—

> "As I came down through Cannobie,
> Through Cannobie, through Cannobie ;
> The summer sun had shut his e'e,
> And loud a lass did sing, O," &c.

The song in Cromek is too rough and unpolished to be modern. In 1793, Ritson first prints the Northumbrian song, in his "*Northumberland Garland,*" and the first verse may be said to be identical with the supposed Jacobite one, with the substitution of the Newcastle Street, Sandgate, for the Edinburgh Cannongate. The second verse of Ritson says "*He wears a blue bonnet.*" Now the blue bonnet was a traditional portion of Scotch dress, and a parallel verse occurs in Cromek, "My love he wears a bonnet." To alter the Ritson and the Cromek version of the song into each other would require but few words, for they are practically the same. Most Scotchmen will, I am aware, claim the Jacobite as the original, and I am sure that, Northumbrians, to a man, will swear by Ritson. I have no wish to do anything, but to lay down evidence. In 1812, Bell in the "*Rhymes of Northern Bards,*" repeats Ritson's version. About 1810-1815, Seield prints the tune in his "*Through Bass,*" and sometime at this period Robert Topliff includes it in his "*Melodies of the Tyne and Wear.*" In the "*Newcastle Chronicle*" mention is made of a MS. book of airs, dated in one place, 1752, which is known to have belonged to a Northumbrian. The Keel Row is noted down in this book, but that alone proves very little, it simply shows that the tune was then popular (we may presume) in Newcastle. Not having seen the book, I am unable to give particulars, but we may conclude that other airs are included which are known to be either Scotch or South Country; nor can we be sure that the date 1752 is the date of entry of the tune. For, as is frequently the case, the book may have taken years to fill up, or have been employed by other persons at a later date, for the same purpose as the original owner. The word "Keel," one might have thought, would settle the disputed question, but, alas! "Keel" is an old Saxon word, and has been used in Scotland as well as Newcastle. I have appended Ritson's and Cromek's versions of the song, for comparison ;—

RITSON'S VERSION.

As I went up Sandgate,
Up Sandgate, up Sandgate,
As I went up Sandgate
  I heard a lassie sing—
Weel may the keel row,
The keel row, the keel row,
Weel may the keel row
  That my laddie's in.

He wears a blue bonnet, etc.,
  A dimple in his chin.
And weel may the keel row, etc.

(Ritson has only these two verses).

CROMEK'S VERSION

As I came down the Canno'gate,
The Canno' gate, the Canno' gate,
As I came down the Canno' gate,
  I heard a lassie sing—
Merry may the keel row,
The keel row, the keel row,
Merry may the keel row,
  The ship that my love's in.

My love has breath of roses, etc.,
With arms of lillie posies,
  To fauld a lassie in.—Merry may, etc.

My love he wears a bonnet, etc.,
A snawy rose upon it,
  A dimple in his chin.—Merry may, etc.

HUMP MY LADY, Page 20, is from a large manuscript collection of Country Dances and other airs, written down by a person in Leeds, about 1820. A hump-backed person used to be called " My Lord," or if a female, " My Lady."

THE TIDE
Songster, 1840, th

The present copy
*for the Pianoforte
Tyne and Wear*,"
DOWN T
a manuscript co
north. (This
country airs,
Robson, in "

evidently the
WE M

ILL THE TIDE COMES IN, Page 20, was a popular Northumbrian tune. In the *Tyne* pted to it—

"While strolling down sweet Sandgate street,
A man-o'-war's blade I chanced to meet:
To the sign of the Ship I hauled him in
To drink a good glass till the tide came in."

ars in a MS., and in "*A Collection of Marches, Quicksteps, Strathspeys, and Reels . . adaptea alvert, Kelso*." Folio. *Circa* 1800. A somewhat different set is in Topliff's "*Melodies of the* It has been long known on the Tyne banks.

WAY, Page 21.—This very singular air is a Northumbrian pipe tune. The present copy is from editor's possession, noted down about 1816, by some person residing at Darlington or in the d by a Darlington printer's label being pasted into the book). The book has many other north are here reproduced. In a rhyming medley composed of the titles of dance and other airs, by *Minstrelsy*," is—

"Saw ye aught of my lad
Gawn up the waggon way?"

he song for the foregoing tune.

IT TILL MY LADY COMES HOME, Page 21.—From the same MS. The air bears great resemblance to one used by Shield in the opera of *Robin Hood,* for the song, " The lasses are mad," &c. As Shield was a north country man, he had doubtless knowledge of the air, and so employed it in the opera.

O! THE WEARY WATERS OF TYNE, Page 22.—This is another Northumbrian air, from the same MS. and like the previous ones, has not, to the editor's knowledge, been before printed.

NEW ROAD TO ALSTON, Page 22.—From the MS. mentioned above. Alston is in a wild and remote district of Cumberland.

PLAINS OF WATERLOO, Page 23.—From the same MS. This air is not to be confounded with the one adapted to a song found on broadsides, and having the same title.

NUMBER ONE, Page 23.—Another good country dance air from the same MS.

FOGGY DEW, Page 24.—From a manuscript, *circa* 1825. It is evidently the air to a ballad found on broadsides, which bearing the same title commences thus—

> " What shepherd was like me so blest
> To tend his fleecy care?
> For welcome unto yonder hills
> I freely did repair.
> 'Twas on a bank of mossy turf,
> Where rosy violets grew,
> 'Twas there I had to lead my flocks,
> Down among the foggy dew."

There is a very beautiful air in Bunting's "*Irish Music*," 1840, having the title "Foggy Dew." It i̶
here given, and could not be used for the above words.

MISS BAKER'S HORNPIPE, Page 24, attained much popularity. It appeared, for I believe
Skillern's Country Dances for 1772. In one of Thompson's collections of about the same period
Hornpipe."

THE KIRKGATE HORNPIPE, Page 25, 1st and 2nd Versions.—These two lively hornpip
greatly popular in Leeds. About fifty years ago a small musical society held its meetings i
Hornpipe" was a great favourite there. The first version is from a manuscript collection dat
another MS. of a little later date. This latter tune is also in the first-named collection, but it
Hornpipe." It is, however, different to an air which now bears that title.

English Country Dances are either in the editor's possession. or have come under his observation. greatly added to, and many books of airs are here omitted which, although they contain dance sections of Country Dances. The dates are given where known, but some latitude must be allowed to quote the date from internal evidence.

-The first collection of Country dance was printed for John Playford, century, and was continued by him seventeen editions for nearly eighty

ed " The English Dancing Master, rules for the dancing of country to each dance, 1651." Contains to

The Dancing Master . . . with 1652." Oblong 12mo.

1657 and 1665, *Third Edition.* These two volumes are classed as one edition.

1670, *Fourth*; 1675, *Fifth*; 1680, *Sixth.*

1686, *Seventh*, with two "additional sheets."

1690, *Eighth*; 1695, *Ninth*, with a second part dated 1696.

1698, *Tenth*, with a second edition of the second part, dated 1698.

1701, *Eleventh*; 1703, *Twelfth*; 1706, *Thirteenth*; 1711, *Fourteenth*; 1713, *Fifteenth.*

1716, *Sixteenth*, with a second volume dated 1718.

1721, *Seventeenth*, with a second and a third volume dated 1728. All after the first being Oblong 12mo.

Each of these editions are essentially different topics, for as airs dropped out of favour they were replaced by ones more popular; and in many instances the titles were changed (in the same tune) as one song was superseded by another. The volumes gradually increased in size, the first having 104 pp. (a tune being on each page); the second, 112 pp.; the eighth, 220 pp.; the twelfth, 252 pp.; and the third volume of the seventeenth, 1728, 200 pp. The title pages were adorned by a small and highly-finished etching, by W. Hollar, depicting a company of ladies and gentlemen in King Charles' costume, dancing. All the music is rudely set up in type, and the dancing directions given to each dance are exceedingly quaint. The British Museum library possesses a complete and unique set of the above volumes, and several editions after the seventh are in the editor's collection.

Walsh, John.—John Walsh, and his son bearing the same Christian name, were contemporaries with Henry Playford, John Playford's son, and did a most extensive business from the beginning to the middle of the 18th century. They issued Country Dances in a similar size and style with Playford's Dancing Master. The earliest the editor has seen is dated 1711, oblong 12mo, but from the advertisement below they appear to have been first printed about 1700.

1711—"Twenty-four new Country Dances for the year 1711, with proper new tunes and figures or directions to each dance, humbly dedicated to ye Honourable Henry I.d. Newport, by his most obedient and most faithful servant, Nathaniel Kynaston. Note—the 1st and 2nd volumes of ye New Country Dancing Master, is reprinted, and may be had where this is sold—*London:* Printed for I. Walsh, servant to Her Majesty, and P. Randall, at the Harp and Hoboy, in Catherine Street; and J. Hare, at the Viol and Flute, in Cornhill." 24 pp., oblong 12mo.

1713—" Twenty-four new Country Dances for the year 1713
. . . the music proper for the violin, hautboy, or flute
. . . *London:* Printed for John Walsh." 24 pp.

1714—" Twenty-four new Country Dances for the year 1714
. . . composed by several authors, all fairly engraven.
Note—the new Country Dancing Master is published,
containing all the country dances for the last ten years.
London: Printed for J. Walsh." 24 pp.

1711—" Twenty-four new Country Dances for the year 1718
. . . dedicated to Richard Warringe . . . by Nat.
Kynaston. Note—there is lately published a new
edition of the great Dance Book, containing 364 country
dances [see below] in a new character and more correct
than the former editions. *London:* Printed for I. Walsh."
24 pp., oblong 12mo.

1718—" The Compleat Country Dancing Master, containing
great variety of dances, both old and new . . . .

London: Printed by H. Meere, for J. Walsh, 1718."
364 pp., 364 dances, oblong 12mo.

1719—" The Second Book of the Compleat Country Dancing
Master, 1719." 376 pp., 376 dances, oblong 12mo.

No date (1730?)—" The new Country Dancing Master,
3rd Book, being a collection of country dances . . .
London: Printed for and sold by I. Walsh." 160pp.,
oblong 12mo.

1731—" The Compleat Country Dancing Master, containing
great variety of dances, both old and new . . . .
London: Printed for and sold by John Walsh,
MDCCXXXI." 150 pp., 300 dances, oblong 12mo.

On the death of John Walsh, *Junior*, date not known,
Wm. Randall became his successor, and on one of his publi-
cations is noticed the above " Compleat Country Dancing
Master, containing above 1,200 dances in 7 vols."

Walsh also issued a collection of Caledonian Country
Dances, in 10 books, but none of these has the editor seen.

Pl... "A Hundr... and Twenty Country
Dances ... being a choice ...llection of the pleasant
and m... out of all th... dance books, both old
and ne... ...1. London, printed for 1. Pippard."
Oblong...

...1720.—"An extraordinary collection
of Pl... ...erry Humours, never before published,
cont... ...es, Jiggs, North Country Frisks ; Morriss's
Bag... ...pes, and Rounds, with several additional
fanci... for all those that play publick. London,
pr... by Daniel Wright, &c." Oblong 8vo.,
36... 70 airs.

...nson, of the Harp and Crown, Cheapside,
... ...mous m... p...blisher, but his name is only
... 1740 to ... In ...55 he advertises what
... ...e Walsh's ... ...ntry Dancing Master,

in 6 vols., consisting of 1200 airs, as well as two volumes of
the Caledonian Dances, possibly he bought either plates or
copies of the book at Walsh's death.

1744—A choice collection of 200 favourite Country Dances
. . . Vol. III., printed for Jno. Johnson. Oblong 8vo.

1748—A choice collection of 200 favourite Country Dances
. . . Vol. 4th, 1748. Oblong 8vo.

1751—Ditto., Volume 6th, 1751. Oblong 8vo.

1755—"Twenty-four Country Dances, with proper tunes
and directions to each dance, and for the year 1755.
John Johnson, London." Oblong 8vo. Advertised on
this—

"Twelve hundred favourite Country Dances, in 6 vols."
"Caledonian Country Dances. Vol. I. and II."
" 2 Collections of Country Dances and Minuets, by
Mr. S. Philpot."
" A collection of Hornpipes for Violin."

Circa 1750—Caledonian Country Dances, with a thorough bass for the harpsichord. Oblong 8vo. John Johnson, London.

Waylett.—1751. "Twenty-four Country Dances for the year 1751. . . . London, printed for H. Waylett . . . . where may be had Twenty-four Dances all by Mr. Thos. Davis." Oblong 8vo.

Kilvington.—17—. Twelve Country Dances, by T. Kilvington, York. Oblong 12mo.

Thompson's Collections of Country Dances are more commonly met with than any other. Sets of twenty-four were published every year, from the middle of the 18th century up to the early part of this. Beside the sets of twenty-four, some collections of two hundred were reprinted from the yearly books. Like Johnson's there were only the trebles of the airs given, and were printed with two dances on each page, on one side of the paper only. Th⸱ ⸱⸱⸱ ⸱e was so usual that, if title page is missing, it is ⸱⸱⸱ ⸱fficult to distinguish the various publishers' sets ⸱⸱⸱ ⸱ther. The original founder of the firm was Peter ⸱⸱⸱ ⸱hose name appears in 1754 as a chocolate-m⸱⸱ ⸱aul's Churchyard, from whence the publications ⸱⸱⸱

Thompson, Peter (1751 ?)—The firs⸱ ⸱⸱⸱ ⸱mp-son's yearly dances the editor has seen is⸱ ⸱⸱⸱ ⸱but starts with Dance No. 97. Calculation wi⸱ ⸱⸱⸱ ⸱rst yearly set of 24 must be dated 1751.

1755—" Twenty-four Country Dances for the ⸱⸱⸱ proper tunes . . . N.B.—The true, ⸱⸱⸱ ⸱s will be published every year in this volum⸱ ⸱⸱⸱ pr. 6d. *London :* Printed for Peter Th⸱ ⸱⸱⸱ Violin and Hautboy, in St. Paul's Churc⸱ ⸱⸱⸱ mences with tune No. 27, ending with ⸱⸱⸱ Oblong 8vo.

1756 to 1800—The ▓▓▓ ▓▓▓▓ ▓▓re issued in sets of twenty-four ▓▓ ▓▓▓▓ ▓▓▓ ▓▓ style and size from 1755 (or 1751 ?) ▓▓ ▓▓▓ ▓▓▓, or a year or two later.

Besid▓▓ ▓▓▓ ▓▓▓ ▓▓▓ly sets of dance books the following were i▓▓▓▓:—

Ci▓ ▓▓ ▓▓▓ ▓▓pson's Complete Collection of 200 ▓▓▓ ▓▓ntry Dances . . . . Vol. I. *London:* ▓▓ ▓▓pson, in St. Paul's Churchyard." Oblong ▓▓▓.

▓▓▓ ▓▓▓—Ditto, Vol. II. Charles and Samuel Thompson. Oblong 8vo.

Cir 1772—Ditto, Vol. III. Charles and Samuel. Ob. 8vo.

Circa 1780 ' Ditto, Vol. IV. Charles and Samuel. Oblong 8vo. Other volumes no doubt followed.

In addition to the violin sets of dances, there were sets of twelve issued with basses for the harpsichord, and these were collected into volumes of about 70 airs. Books of minuets and of hornpipes were also printed, all in the oblong octavo shape.

In the Yearly Dances for 1759, Peter Thompson's name on title page was changed to Thompson & Son, and in 1762 an "s" was added to Son. The sons were Charles and Samuel, and their names soon after appear alone, the father having either died or retired. In 1779 the firm was Samuel and Ann, evidently the widow of Charles; and in 1781 to 1795 it is Samuel, Ann, and Peter, the latter being doubtless a son of Charles or Samuel. After 1795 Henry replaces Peter, and in 1796 it is Henry and Ann; ultimately, in 1800 Henry Thompson's name alone appears. The firm carried on business at 75, St. Paul's Churchyard, and between 1800 and 1806 it was passed over to Button & Purday, which, after a few years, became Button & Whitaker, the address being still 75, St. Paul's Churchyard.

Straight & Skillern, 1768—" Twenty-four Country Dances for the year 1768 . . . *London :* Printed for T. Straight & Skillern, Great Russell St., Covent Garden." Oblong 8vo.

1775—" Two Hundred and Four favourite Country Dances . . . Vol. I. *London :* Printed for Straight & Skillern, St. Martin's Lane " (This is the Yearly Dances from 1768 to 1775). Oblong 8vo.

1788 to 1791—" Twenty-four new Country Dances, for 1788 [and to 1791] . . . *London :* T. Skillern, 17, St. Martin's Lane." Oblong 8vo.

Circa 1810—"A favourite collection of popular Country Dances . . . *London :* Skillern & Challoner, 25, Greek St., Soho (removed from St. Martin's Lane)." No. 10. Folio, 4 pp.

Rutherford, *circa* 1770—" Rutherford's Compleat Collection of the most celebrated Country Dances, both Old and New. . . . Printed and sold by David Rutherford . . ." (No date). Oblong 8vo.

Randall, 1772—" Twenty-four Country Dances, for the year 1772. . . . *London :* Wm. Randall, successor to the late Mr. Walsh." Oblong 8vo.

Longman, Lukey, & Co., 1772—" Twenty-four Country Dances, for the year 1772. . . . *London :* Longman, Lukey, & Co." Oblong 8vo.

Werner, 1779—" For the year 1779, Four New Minuets, with Six Favourite Cotillions. . . Francis Werner." Oblong 4to.

1782—" Book XV., for the year 1782, Twelve New Country Dances. . . . Francis Werner." Oblong 16mo.

1783 – Book XVI., for the year 1783, ditto.

M iny others by Werner (who died before 1798, and was succeeded by Jno. Fentum) of little interest.

Cahusac

year 1785. .

1790 Ditt

Bu

untry Dances, for the

. long 8vo.

Oblong 8vo.

enth Book, for the year 1786.

s and Country Dances . . .

on : J. Preston." Oblong 16mo.

" Twenty-four Country Dances, for the

ndon : J. Preston, where may be had

'Collection of the favourite Cotillions."

reston's Twenty-four Country Dances, for the year

94." Oblong 8vo.

1800—" Preston's Selection of the most Favourite Country Dances, Reels, etc, Book 3rd." Oblong 4to.

Fentum, 1789 – For the year 1789, Eight Cotillions and Six Country Dances. *London :* Jno. Fentum." Oblong 4to.

1795—" For the year 1795, a Collection of all the Favourite Dances. . . . John Fentum." Oblong 4to.

1795—" Sixteen new Country Dances . . . John Fentum." Oblong 4to.

1796—" Sixteen new Country Dances. Fentum." Oblong 4to.

1796—" A Collection of all the Favourite Dances. Fentum." Oblong 4to.

1798 Ditto. Oblong 4to.

1798— Sixteen new Country Dances . . . by Jno. Fentum, who intends continuing the work in the same manner as the late F. Werner." Oblong 4to.

1810—" Fentum's Annual Collection of Twenty-four Favourite Dances for the year 1810." Oblong 8vo.

Hoffman, 1796—" Fourteen Country Dances, for the year 1796 . . by R. Hoffman." Oblong 4to.

Platts, M., *circa* 1796—"Cotillions and Country Dances. M. Platts. Book No. 22." Oblong 4to.

1798—"Book 25, for the year 1798, of Strathspey Reels, Waltzes, and Irish Jiggs, by Martin Platts. *London:* Longman, Broderip." Oblong 4to.

Circa 1800 to 1810—"Platts' Original and Popular Dances." (Nos. 1 to 34). The first 24 forming Vol. I. and II. Folio.

Harbour, 1796—"A Selection of the most admired Country Dances . . . by J. Harbour." Oblong 4to.

"A 2nd selection," ditto. Oblong 4to.

(These two not dated, but ascertained to have been published both in 1796).

Circa 1800—"Jacob Harbour's third book of new and favourite Country Dances," etc. Oblong 4to.

Lintern, 1797—"Ten Country Dances and Four Cotil- lions . . . for the Lintern's Music Wareho   d sold at J. W.   4to.

Goulding, 1797—"Tw   ces, for the year 1797. . . . *London:*

1800 to 1816—"Goulding, D'Almai Collection of Country Dances, 38." Folio.

(Nos. 1 to 25 form the first volume. 3 pp. music).

1810—"Twenty-four Country Dances, for the Goulding, Phipps, & D'Almaine." Oblong 8vo.

1812—Ditto. Oblong 8vo.

1815 to 1820—"Goulding & Co.'s Collection of New a Favourite Country Dances and Reels . . . arranged for the pianoforte, flute . . . by John Parry." (Six vols oblong 4to.)

1839—"D'Almaine & Co.'s New Country Dances, for the year 1839." Oblong 8vo.
1841—Ditto. Oblong 8vo.

Campbell, *circa* 1790 to 1815—"Campbell's 1st Book of New and Favourite Country Dances." Oblong 4to. (Extends to at least the 27th book, each book having from 22 pp. to 16 pp.)

Harrison, *circa* 1800—Thirty Popular Airs, Reels, Dances, etc." (In Pianoforte Magazine, vol. 16). 8vo.

Bland & Weller, *circa* 1800—"Bland & Weller's New Collection of Scotch Dances. . . . Book III." Oblong 4to.

Metralcourt, *circa* 1800—"Twenty-four Country Dances . . . by Charles Metralcourt. . . . Printed for the author, and sold by Longman & Broderip and T. Skillern." Oblong 4to.

Walker, *circa* 1800 to 1815—"Walker's Collection of Favourite Dances, for the pianoforte or violin. No. 1 to 38." (or more; No. 16 is "for the year 1808.") Folio.

Astor, 1803—"Astor's Twenty-four Country Dances, for the year 1803." Oblong 8vo.
1818—"Astor & Harwood's Twenty-four Country Dances, for the year 1818." Oblong 8vo.

Andrews, *circa* 1805—"Five Favourite Dances, for the pianoforte or violin." Nos. 1 to 26. Folio.

Button & Whitaker, *circa* 1805 to 1810—"No. 1 (to 15), Button & Whitaker's selection of Dances, Reels, and Waltzes." Folio.

Dale, *circa* 1805 to 1812—Dale's Collection of Reels and Dances," Nos. 1 to 25 (at least). Folio.

Longman & Broderip, *circa* 1805—"Longman & Broderip's Fourth Selection of the most Favourite Country Dances. . . . ." Oblong 4to.

Kotswora, *circa* 1805—" Twelve Country Dances and Cotillions, by Kotswora." Oblong 8vo.

Balls, *circa* 1809—" Balls' Collection of Popular Country Dances. . . . *London :* J. Balls, 408, Oxford Street." (Nos. 1, 2, 3). Folio.

Hodsall, 1810—" Hodsall's Annual Collection of Twenty-four Favourite Country Dances . . for the year 1810." Oblong 8vo.

Halliday, *circa* 1810—" Halliday & Co.'s Collection of New Dances." Folio.

Gerock's, 1812—" C. Gerock's Annual Collection of Twenty-four Country Dances, for the year 1812." Oblong 8vo. 1813—Ditto. Oblong 8vo.

Shade, *circa* 1815—" Collection of Dances, No. 7. *London :* Printed for G. Shade." Folio.

Wilson, 1816—" Companion to the Ball Room, a Collection of Country Dances, Reels, etc., edited by Thomas Wilson."

Hale, *circa* 1816—" Hale's Selection of Popular Waltzes and Dances. . . Cheltenham. Book I." Oblong 4to.

Monro, 1817—" For the year 1817, Monro's Annual Set of Country Dances." Oblong 8vo. 1820 and 1821—Ditto. 1834—Ditto.

Draper, 1818—" Draper's Collection of Favourite Waltzes for the year 1818. Printed by G. Shade." Folio.

Major, 1820—" Major's Annual Collection of Twenty-four of the most fashionable Country Dances . . . 1820." Oblong 8vo.

Parry, *circa* 1820—" Parry's Original Country Dances, for the violin. . . ." Folio, 2 pp.

1825—" Analysis of the London Ball Room." Published by Tegg. 8vo

Townsend. *cir.* 1830—" Twenty-four Favourite Country Dances, for the German flute. J. Townsend, Manchester." Oblong 8vo.

Clementi, 1836 —" Clementi & Co.'s Dances, Waltzes, and Quadrilles, for the year 1836." Oblong 8vo.

———o———

. English Dance collections were issued in Dublin, in folio sheets. *Some few are as follows :—*

" E Lee's Collection of Country Dances for the present year." (*Circa* 1800.)

" Mrs. Parker's much-admired Selections of Strathspeys and Reels, published by Hime." (*Circa* 1800).

" Hime's collection of Country Dances, No. 1 to 10." (No. 6 is " for 1810.")

Dance Sheets issued by F. Rhames and his successor, P. Alday. (*Circa* 1790—1800).

Finis.

WS - #0042 - 100323 - C0 - 229/152/5 - PB - 9780331881462 - Gloss Lamination